The Kaabah

MY FIRST BOOK ABOUT THE SACRED HOUSE

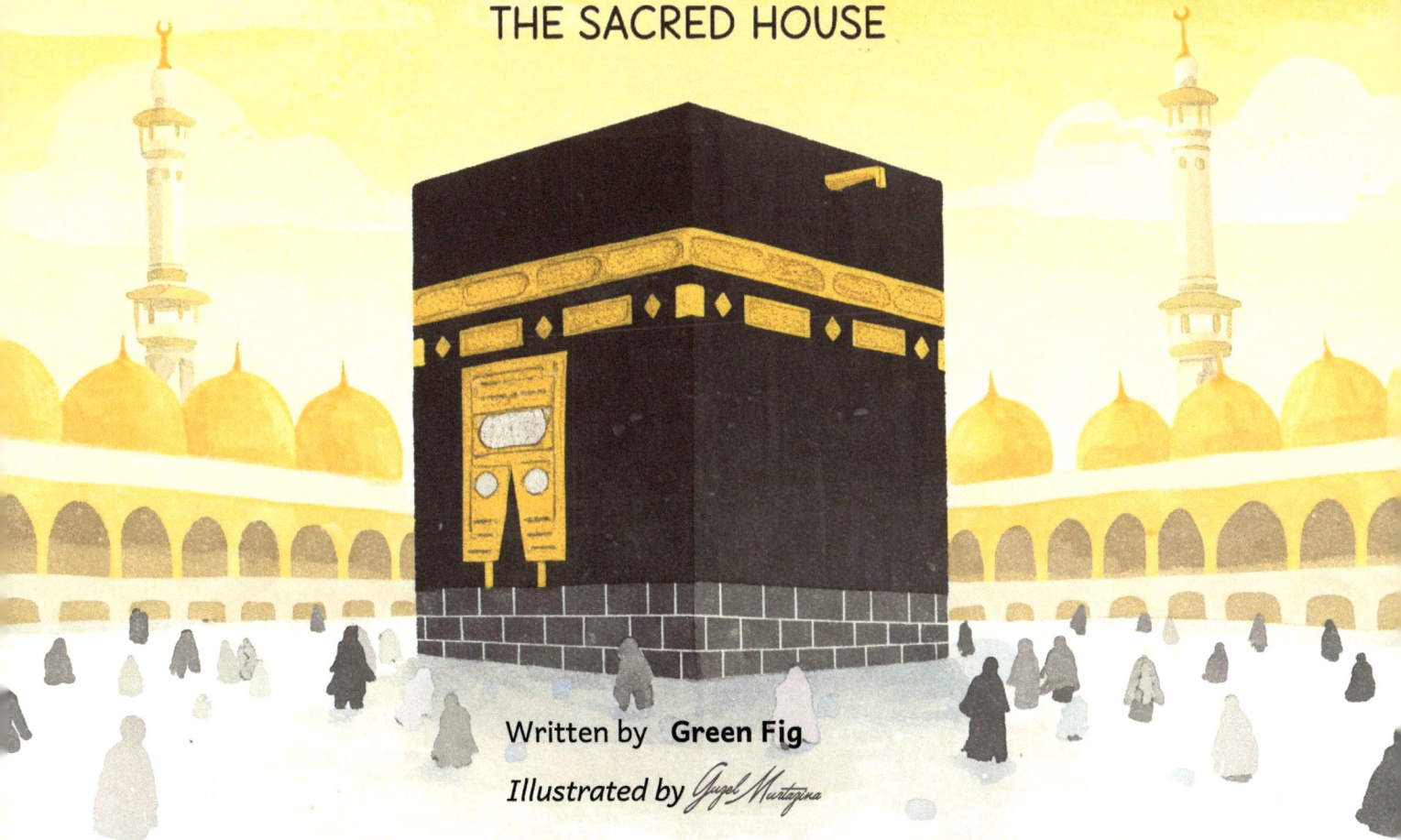

Written by **Green Fig**

Illustrated by *Guzel Murtazina*

Name:

....

....

Green Fig
Proud Muslim Kids

ISBN: 978-1953836755
Publisher: Green Fig
Pennsylvania, USA
gogreenfig.com

Dear Parents & Educators

Green Fig is happy to introduce the first book from Our Heritage Series—**The Ka'bah: My First Book about the Sacred House.** The Ka'bah is not just a structure of stone—it is the very first house built for the worship of Allāh on Earth. Mentioned in the Qur'an and honored by millions of Muslims around the world, it is a symbol of unity and devotion. Teaching children about the Ka'bah connects them to the heart of our faith and helps them appreciate the significance of this sacred place.

Allāh says in the Qur'an:

$$إِنَّ أَوَّلَ بَيْتٍ وُضِعَ لِلنَّاسِ لَلَّذِي بِبَكَّةَ مُبَارَكًا وَهُدًى لِّلْعَالَمِينَ$$

"Indeed, the first House [of worship] established for mankind was that at Bakkah [Makkah]—blessed and a guidance for the worlds."
 (Surah Āl 'Imrān 3:96)

This book introduces young readers to the Ka'bah's location, structure, and special features in a simple and engaging way. By learning these details early, children grow up with a love and reverence for the Ka'bah, longing to one day visit it and pray in its mosque, just like millions of believers before them.

Green Fig Team

The **Kaabah** is a very blessed place. It is the most loved building in the whole world.

Kaabah
الكَعْبَة

Wherever Muslims are in the world, they turn to face the Kaabah when they pray. This special direction is called the **Qiblah**.

Qiblah
القِبْلَة

The Kaabah is in **Makkah**,
the best city on Earth

Makkah
مَكَّة

It stands in the middle of a great mosque called **Al-Masjid al-Ḥarām**.

Al-Masjid Al-Ḥarām

المَسْجِد الحَرام

A long time ago, the Kaabah was the first house built to worship Allāh ﷻ.

It was first built at the time of **Prophet Adam** ﷺ

Later, **Prophet Ibrahim** ﷺ and his son **Isma'il** ﷺ rebuilt the Kaabah.

They raised its walls with strong stones.

The Kaabah is shaped like a **cube**.

It has four sides.

The Kaabah has four **corners**. Each corner is called a **Rukun** and each one has a special name.

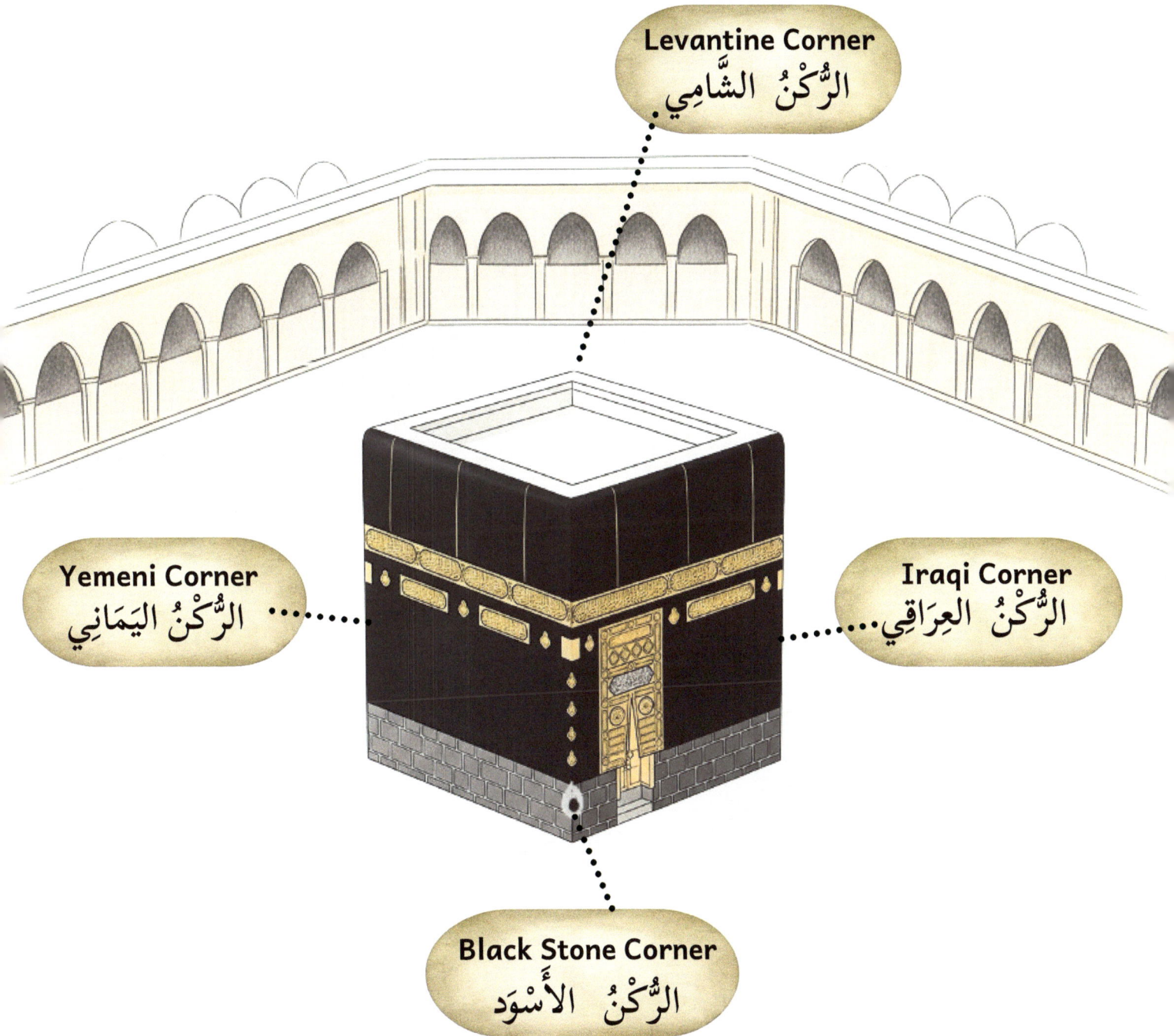

Levantine Corner
الرُّكْنُ الشَّامِي

Yemeni Corner
الرُّكْنُ اليَمَانِي

Iraqi Corner
الرُّكْنُ العِرَاقِي

Black Stone Corner
الرُّكْنُ الأَسْوَد

The most famous corner is where the **Black Stone** sits.

Black Stone
الحَجَر الأَسْوَد

The **Black Stone** came from **Paradise**. It was **white**, but turned **black** after many people touched it.

At the base of the Kaabah is a marble part called the **Shadharwān**. It looks like a bench around the bottom.

Shadharwān
الشَّاذَرْوَان

The Kaabah has a **Golden Door**. It is made of real gold and shines brightly in the sunlight. The door sits high up and is opened only on special days, like when the Kaabah is cleaned.

Golden Door

بَابُ الْكَعْبَةِ الذَّهَبِي

There is a golden spout on the roof called the **Meezāb**

It pours rainwater off the roof. It is very special to make dua' under it.

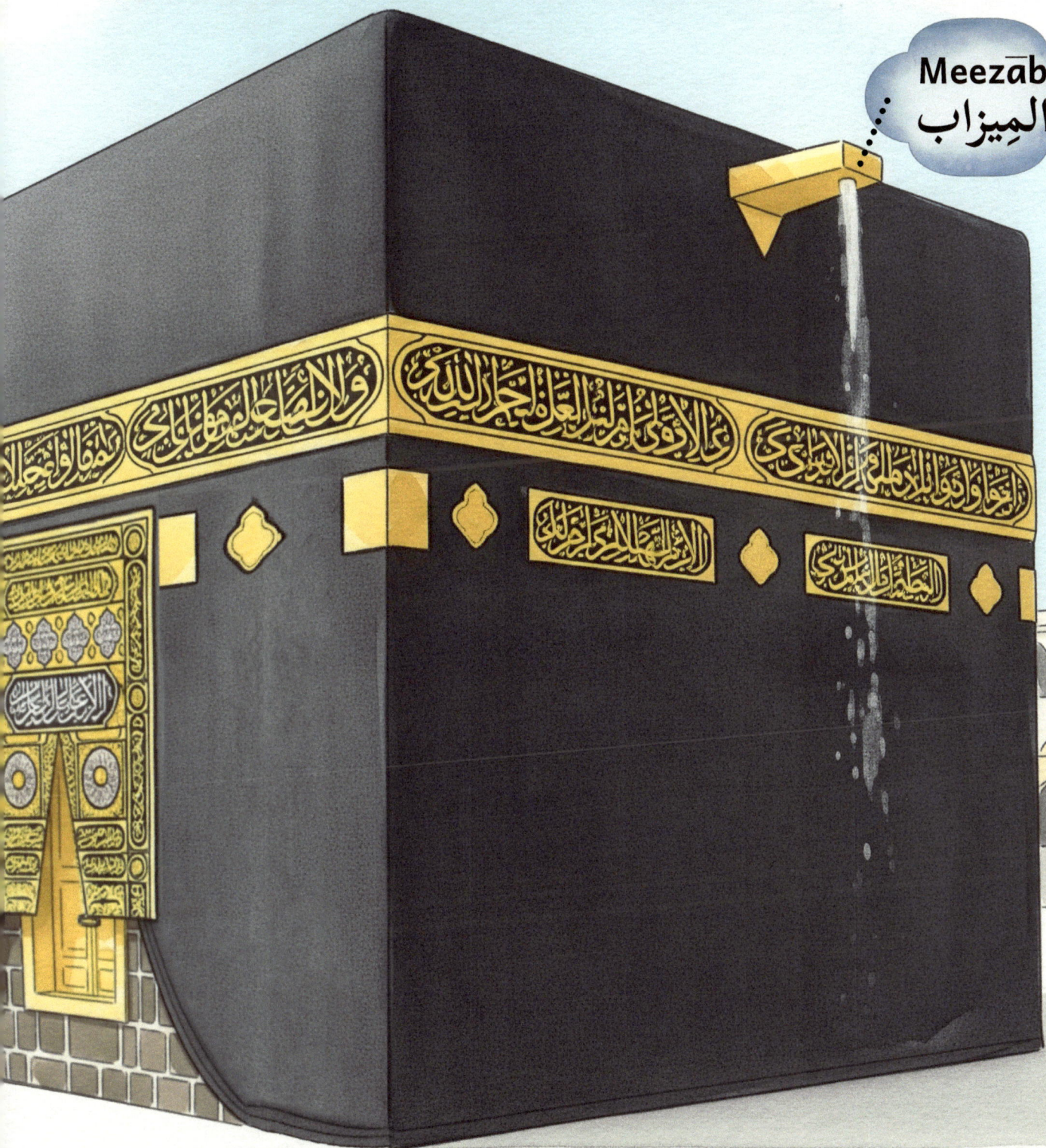

Next to the Kaabah is a curved white wall. The space inside it is called **<u>H</u>ijr Isma'il**.

It is part of the Kaabah.

People love to pray there.

It is a special place.

Hijr Isma'il
حِجْر إِسْمَاعِيل

A long time ago, the Kaabah was bigger. But when it was rebuilt there were not **enough stones**. So the people built a wall to show the part that was left out. That place was called <u>H</u>**ijr Isma'il**.

The Kaabah is covered with a black cloth called the **Kiswah**. It's decorated with verses from the **Qur'an** in gold and silver.

Every year, the Kiswah is changed during the **<u>H</u>ajj** season. **<u>H</u>ajj** is a special journey called **piligrimage**. Muslims from all over the world make to **Makkah** every year.

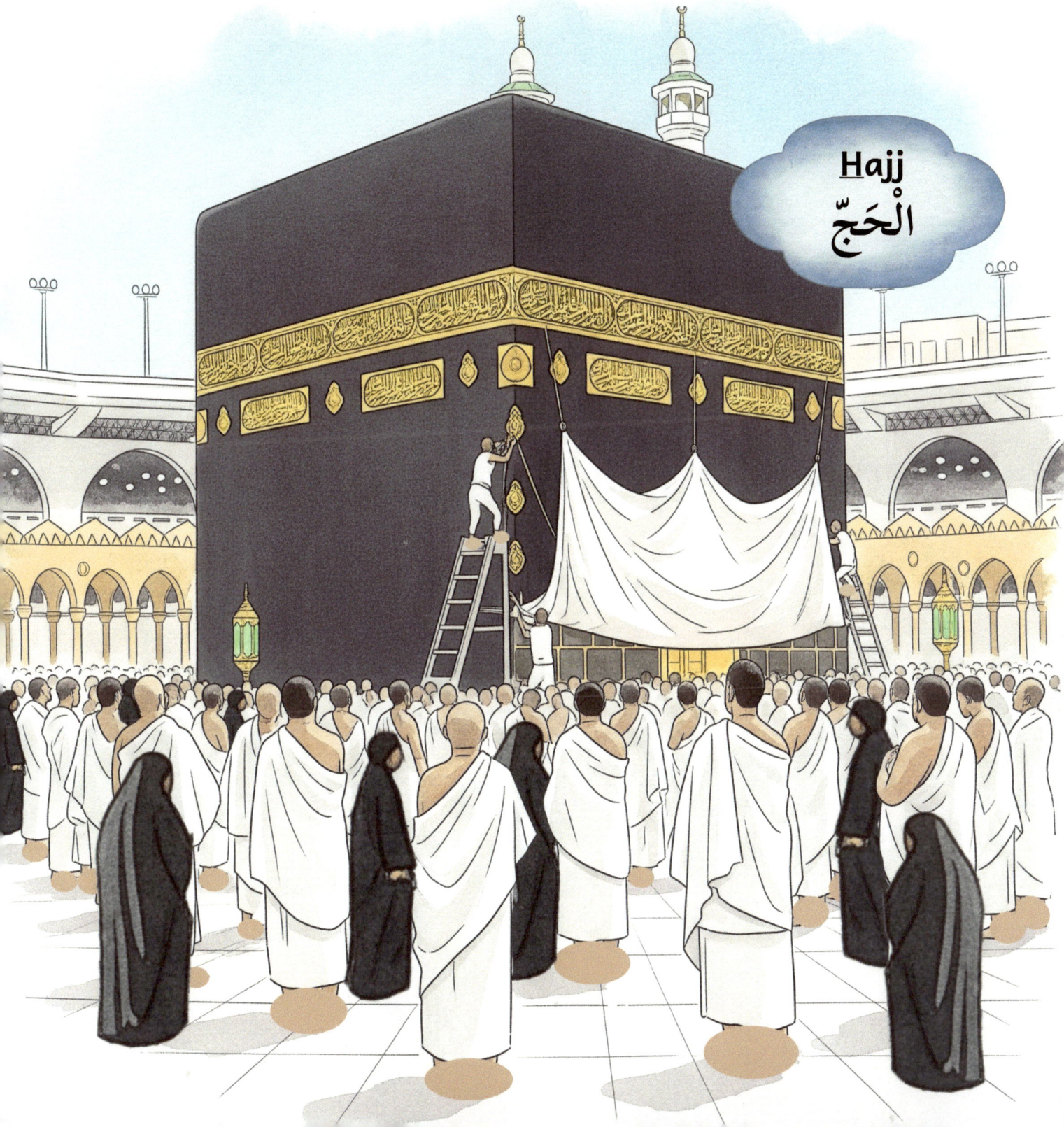

Hajj
الْحَجّ

When Muslims go to **H̲ajj**, they walk around the **Kaabah seven times**. This is called **T̲awāf**.

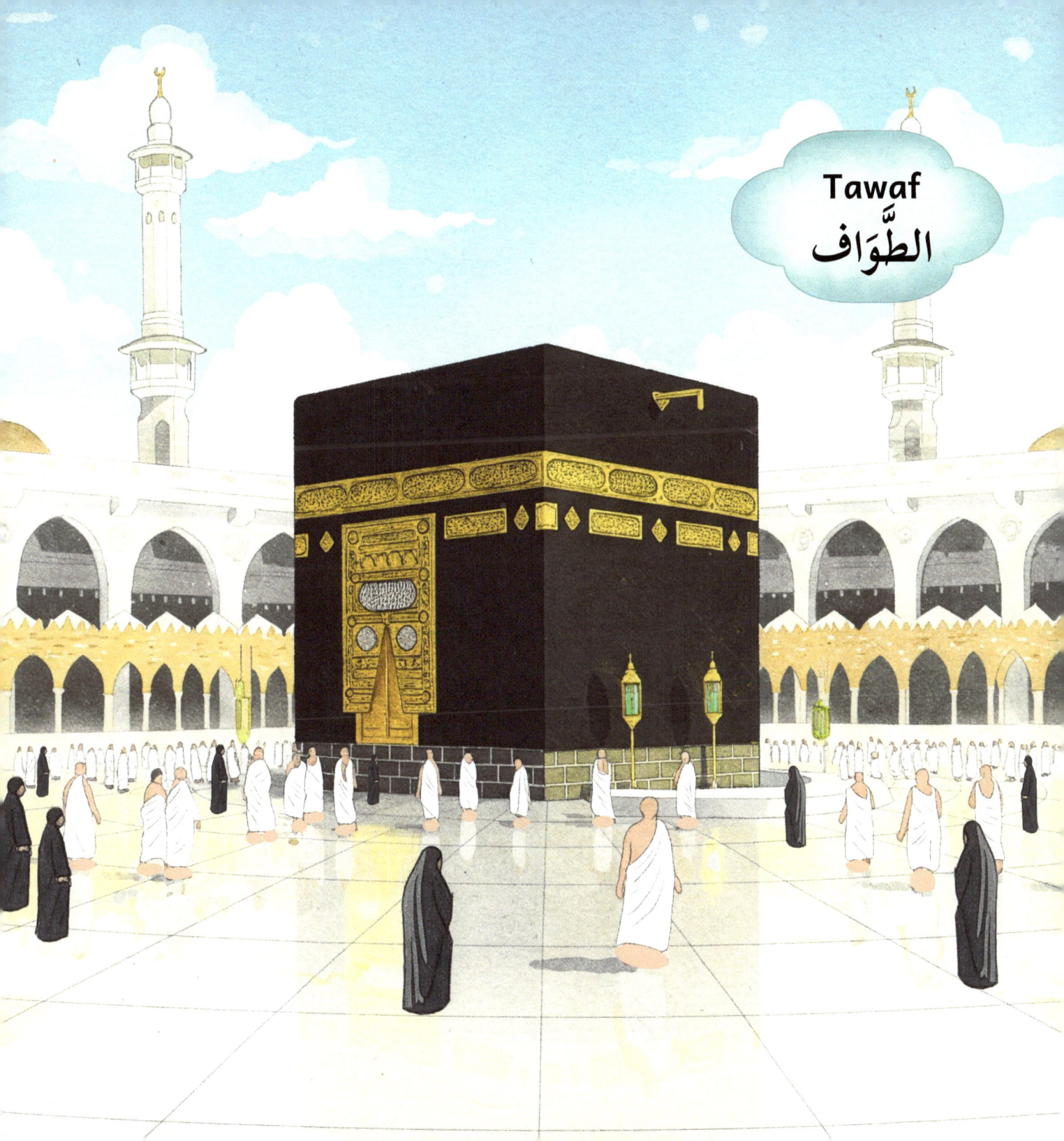

Tawaf
الطَّوَاف

Near the Kaabah is a stone called **Maqām Ibrahim**. It's where Prophet Ibrahim ﷺ stood while building the Kaabah. Today, it sits a little away from the Kaabah and is covered in a golden

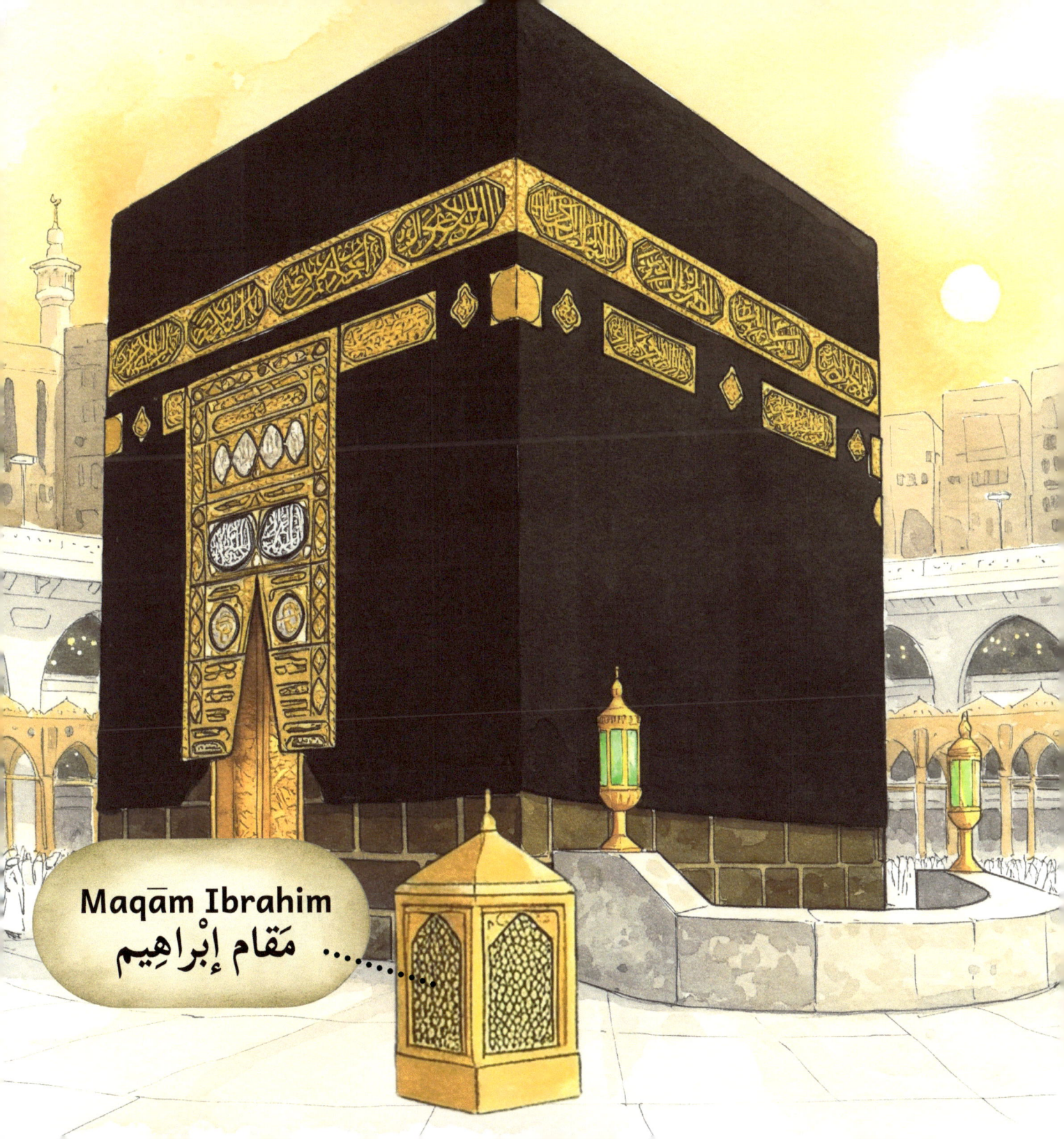

Maqām Ibrahim
مَقام إِبْراهِيم ....

We love the Kaabah-our Qiblah.

It is the most loved place on earth. It reminds us to pray, to worship **Allāh** ﷻ. and stay united as one Ummah. One day I want to go there.

O Allāh, let me visit Your Sacred House.

www.ingramcontent.com/pod-product-compliance
Lightning Source LLC
LaVergne TN
LVHW072130070426
835513LV00002B/51